Acting Edition

THE ONE-ACT PLAY THAT GOES WRONG

BY HENRY LEWIS
JONATHAN SAYER
& HENRY SHIELDS

DPS
DRAMATISTS PLAY SERVICE

ISBN 978-0-8222-4199-7
www.dramatists.com
www.concordtheatricals.com

THE ONE-ACT PLAY THAT GOES WRONG was first presented by Mischief Theatre under the title *The Murder Before Christmas* on December 4, 2012, at the Old Red Lion Theatre, Islington, London. It was directed by Mark Bell, the designer was Henry Lewis, the lighting design was by Scott Pryce-Jones, the costume design was by Bryony Myers, the stage manager was Thomas Platt, and the general manager was Nicholas Thompson. The cast was as follows:

CHRIS .... Henry Shields
JONATHAN .... Stephen Leask
ROBERT .... Henry Lewis
DENNIS .... Jonathan Sayer
SANDRA .... Charlie Russell
MAX .... Dave Hearn
ANNIE .... Nancy Wallinger
TREVOR .... Rob Falconer

The production then extended under the title THE PLAY THAT GOES WRONG on March 12, 2013, with the following cast changes:

JONATHAN .... Henry Lewis
ROBERT .... Greg Tannahill
SANDRA .... Lotti Maddox

The production then transferred to Trafalgar Studios on April 30, 2013, with the following cast changes:

JONATHAN .... Joshua Elliott
ROBERT .... Henry Lewis

The production extended at Trafalgar Studios with the following cast change:

JONATHAN .... Greg Tannahill

It subsequently opened in a two-act version under the title THE PLAY THAT GOES WRONG at the Duchess Theatre, London, a Nimax Theatre, on September 14, 2014. Kenny Wax & Stage Presence presented the Mischief Theatre production. It was directed by Mark Bell, the set design was by Nigel Hook, the lighting design was by Ric Mountjoy, the costume design was by Roberto Surace, the original music was by Rob Falconer, and the sound design was by Andy Johnson. The opening night cast was as follows:

TREVOR .... Rob Falconer
CHRIS .... Henry Shields
JONATHAN .... Greg Tannahill
ROBERT .... Henry Lewis
DENNIS .... Jonathan Sayer
SANDRA .... Charlie Russell
MAX .... Dave Hearn
ANNIE .... Nancy Wallinger
JILL & FEMALE UNDERSTUDY .... Alys Metcalf
PHIL & MALE UNDERSTUDY .... Leonard Cook

THE PLAY THAT GOES WRONG opened on Broadway at the Lyceum Theatre, a Shubert Theatre, in April 2017. It was produced by Kevin McCollum, J.J. Abrams, Kenny Wax, Stage Presence Ltd., Catherine Schreiber, Ken Davenport, Double Gemini Productions/deRoy-Brunish, Damian Arnold/TC Beech, Greenleaf Productions/Bard-Roth, Martian Entertainment/Jack Lane/John Yonover, Lucas McMahon, and Mischief Theatre. It was directed by Mark Bell, the scenic design was by Nigel Hook, the costume design was by Roberto Surace, the lighting design was by Ric Mountjoy, the sound design was by Andrew Johnson, the associate costume designer was Lisa Zinni, the associate lighting designer was Jeremy Cunningham, and the associate sound designer was Beth Lake. The opening night cast was as follows:

TREVOR .... Rob Falconer
MAX .... Dave Hearn
ROBERT .... Henry Lewis
SANDRA .... Charlie Russell
DENNIS .... Jonathan Sayer
CHRIS .... Henry Shields
JONATHAN .... Greg Tannahill
ANNIE .... Nancy Zamit
UNDERSTUDIES .... Matthew Cavendish (CHRIS, DENNIS, JONATHAN, MAX, TREVOR)
Bryony Corrigan (ANNIE, SANDRA)
Adam Daveline (CHRIS, DENNIS, MAX, ROBERT, TREVOR)
Jonathan Fielding (CHRIS, DENNIS, JONATHAN, MAX, ROBERT)
Amelia McClain (ANNIE, SANDRA, TREVOR)
Greg Tannahill (ROBERT)
Michael Thatcher (JONATHAN, ROBERT, TREVOR)

CHARACTERS

As with any play within a play, you have the slight complication of the characters of the actors doing the play within the play and the characters within the play within the play. To try and make it a little simpler, the names are laid out below in two lists: firstly the actors, the members of The Cornley Polytechnic Drama Society who are putting on the play, and secondly the characters of the play The Murder at Haversham Manor. *The text always specifies and refers to the actors rather than the characters.*

MEMBERS OF THE CORNLEY POLYTECHNIC DRAMA SOCIETY
(in order of appearance)

ANNIE is the company's stage manager. American accent.

TREVOR is the company's lighting and sound operator. American accent.

CHRIS is the head of the drama society, directed the play and plays Inspector Carter.

JONATHAN plays Charles Haversham.

ROBERT plays Thomas Colleymoore.

DENNIS plays Perkins.

MAX plays Cecil Haversham.

SANDRA plays Florence Colleymoore.

The action takes place on opening night of The Cornley Polytechnic Drama Society's production of the murder mystery play The Murder at Haversham Manor, *written by Susie H. K. Brideswell.*

Characters in *The Murder at Haversham Manor*

(in order of appearance)

CHARLES HAVERSHAM, deceased.

THOMAS COLLEYMOORE, Charles' old school friend.

PERKINS, Charles' butler.

CECIL HAVERSHAM, Charles' brother.

FLORENCE COLLEYMOORE, Charles' fiancée and Thomas' sister.

INSPECTOR CARTER, an esteemed local inspector.

The action takes place in Charles' private room at Haversham Manor on the evening of Charles and Florence's engagement party. Winter 1922.

PRODUCTION NOTES

(a few notes from the writers about the piece)

The stage direction "*vamp*" denotes improvised dialogue to cover something. In our experience less is always more with this, but also finding believable improvised lines for your versions of the actors is important, and for that reason we haven't included specifics from the original production.

An underlined letter in the text indicates a mispronunciation in that part of the word.

/ denotes the next line beginning over the current line.

In the very first run of the show, we finished it with a 5–8 minute improvised Q&A session, where the audience could ask the actors questions about the performance. For various reasons this may or may not be appropriate for different productions, but it was a nice way to allow the audience to meet the actors rather than see them only through the *Haversham Manor* characters. Of course in the Q&A none of the actors (except possibly Chris) realise that it's gone that wrong.

There is a little specified in the text about preshow activity while the audience is coming in. More could be added to what is written in stage direction to suit the space and to give brief glimpses of some of the actors to help set up offstage relationships. Any action should remain subtle and in low light, allowing audience conversation to flow over it.

THE ONE-ACT PLAY THAT GOES WRONG

The stage is set with a low-budget (but not terrible) depiction of the private rooms of a young wealthy man of the time. The back wall consists of three set flats: one stage left with a door in it, one stage right with a fireplace half-painted onto it, and one in the centre with a window in it, with curtains drawn in front of it.

A clock and barometer hang either side of the door. A chaise longue stands in the centre of the stage, a drinks trolley (not quite of the period) stands stage left, and a small table with a telephone and a vase on it downstage right. A coal scuttle sits beside the fireplace and other various set dressings from different periods of history fill the space.

As the audience enter, Annie (the stage manager) kneels by the bottom of the flat, trying to affix the mantelpiece onto the fireplace with no success.

House music drops to a lower level as Trevor (the lighting and sound operator) moves to the front of the stage.

TREVOR. Good evening ladies and gentlemen. A couple of announcements; Number one; turn your phones off. Secondly, if anyone finds a Duran Duran* CD box set in the auditorium, I need that back, please hand it to me at the end of the performance. Enjoy the show.

Trevor exits to the lighting box.

Clearance.

Trevor cues the lights to fade to black. Annie still hasn't finished the mantelpiece. Chris enters from around the back of the flats in the darkness.

* If music by a different band is used on pages 33 and 46, change "Duran Duran" appropriately.

CHRIS. Leave it. Just leave it.

ANNIE. We need…

CHRIS. We haven't got time.

Annie hurries off behind the flat, taking the mantelpiece and tools with her. Spotlight comes up, Chris hurries into it.

Good evening ladies and gentlemen and welcome to The Cornley Polytechnic Drama Society's spring production of *The Murder at Haversham Manor.*

I would like to personally welcome you to what will be my directorial debut, and my first production as head of the drama society.

We are particularly excited to present this play because, for the first time in the society's history, we have managed to find a play that fits the company's numbers perfectly. If we're honest a lack of numbers has hampered past productions. Last year's Chekhov play, *Two Sisters.* Or last Christmas' *The Lion and the Wardrobe*, and of course our summer musical, *Cat.*

It may interest you to know that this will also be the first time the society has been able to stage a play of this scale. There's no question that usually we have to contend with a small budget, such as in last year's presentation of Roald Dahl's *James and the Peach.* Of course, during the run of that particular show the peach went off, and we were forced to present a hastily devised alternative entitled *James! Where's Your Peach?*

Finally we can afford to stage a play as it should be, and which, may I say, has been exceptionally well cast. I'm sure no one will forget the problems we've faced with casting before, such as our presentation of *Snow White and the Tall, Broad Gentlemen*, or indeed our previous year's pantomime, another Disney classic: *Ugly…and the Beast.*

But now, on with the main event, which I am confident will be our best show yet! So without further ado, please put your hands together for Susie H. K. Brideswell's thrilling whodunit—*The Murder at Haversham Manor.*

Chris exits around the flats and the stage lights fade to black. Jonathan (playing Charles Haversham) enters through the darkness. He loudly collides with the drinks trolley.

JONATHAN. *(Under his breath.)* Shit.

The lights suddenly come up on Jonathan. He freezes. The lights go out again. Jonathan takes up his position, dead, on the chaise longue, arm outstretched onto the floor. The lights come up again, just before he's fully in position. Robert (playing Thomas Colleymoore) and Dennis (playing Perkins the butler) can be heard off, approaching the door.

ROBERT. *(Off.)* Charley! Are you ready? We're all waiting downstairs to raise a glass to your engagement! Charley?

Robert knocks on the door.

(Off.) Come along now Charley, you've been in there for hours now. If I didn't know better I'd say you were having second thoughts about the wedding! *(Chuckle.)* Hang it all Charley, if you won't come out, I'll come in! *(Tries handle.)* Damn it! He's locked the door! Hand me those keys, Perkins!

DENNIS. *(Off.)* Here they are, Mr. Colleymoore!

ROBERT. *(Off.)* Thank you Perkins. Let's get this door open. We're coming in, Charley! We're coming in!

Robert goes to open the door, but it won't budge.

(Off.) There we are. We're in.

Robert and Dennis dart around the side of the set to enter.

But, what's this? Charles, unconscious?

DENNIS. Asleep surely, Mr. Colleymoore?

ROBERT. Damn it, Perkins, I hope so.

DENNIS. I'll take his pulse!

ROBERT. Blast! I knew something was wrong, it's so unlike Charles to disappear like this!

DENNIS. Sir! He's dead!

Lights snap to red. Dramatic musical spike. Lights snap back to general state.

ROBERT. *Dead?!* Damn it Perkins, he can't be! He's my closest friend!

DENNIS. He's not breathing sir and there's no hint of a heartbeat!

ROBERT. I'm dumbfounded! He was right as rain an hour ago.

Robert crosses in front of the chaise longue, treading on Jonathan's outstretched hand.

DENNIS. I don't understand. He was as fit as a fiddle. He can't be dead. It doesn't make sense.

ROBERT. Of course it makes sense. He's been murdered!

Lights change to red again. The same dramatic musical spike. Lights change back to general state.

Good God; where's Florence?

DENNIS. In the dining room sir, shall I fetch her?

ROBERT. Not yet! The last thing we need is for her to have one of her hysterical episodes.

DENNIS. Yes, sir. Do you think it was murder Mr. Colleymoore? Or do you think perhaps it was suicide?

ROBERT. Suicide! Charley? Not possible! There never was a man with more zest for life than Charley! He was young, rich and soon to be married, why on earth would he commit suicide?

DENNIS. But why on earth would anyone murder him, sir? Charles was such a good man. Generous, kind, a true... *(Reads the word from his hand and mispronounces it.)* philanthropist. He never had an enemy in his life.

ROBERT. Until today it seems. Damn it, Perkins! Charles Haversham was murdered in cold blood in this very room on this very day, in this very room! *(Realises his mistake.)*

DENNIS. Shall I telephone the police, Mr. Colleymoore?

ROBERT. The police? They wouldn't make it out here for days in this snowstorm.

Robert opens the curtains to reveal falling paper snowflakes. He closes the curtains again.

I'll telephone Inspector Carter, he lives just the other side of the village. *(Picks up receiver.)* He'll be here in next to no time. Hand me the receiver, Perkins.

Robert realises he already has the receiver.

Thank you, Perkins.

Dennis sits on Jonathan's leg.

Good Evening. Give me Inspector Carter! …I know it's late!… Damn it, I don't care about the weather. There's been a murder! Someone's murdered Charles Haversham!

Lights change to blue. A much longer dramatic musical spike. Lights change back to general state.

That's right! Thank you. *(Hangs up.)* He's on his way.

DENNIS. Inspector Carter?

ROBERT. They say he's the best damn inspector in the district, he'll crack this case and quick.

DENNIS. Very good sir and what shall I do?

ROBERT. Lock every door man!

Robert crosses the stage again. Jonathan sharply moves his hand out of the way of Robert's foot. Jonathan replaces his hand. Dennis treads on it.

Not a soul gets out of Haversham Manor until the killer is found!

DENNIS. At once, sir.

ROBERT. …and assemble everyone in here.

DENNIS. Right away sir!

Dennis goes to leave through the door, but it still won't budge. He exits around the side.

ROBERT. Good God! Just an hour into the engagement party and already there's been a murder! *(Turns sharply to the door.)* Florence!

Sandra tries to get through the door.

SANDRA. *(Off.)* Charley!

ROBERT. Get out Florence! You can't be in here.

SANDRA. *(Off.)* No! I can't believe what I'm seeing.

Sandra cannot get through the door so pokes her head around through the tabs at the side of the scenery.

My god he looks so frail lying there.

ROBERT. I'm sorry Florence, it's a shock to all of us.

SANDRA. His skin is cold to the touch.

ROBERT. No, don't touch him Florence!

SANDRA. I must!

ROBERT. You mustn't!

SANDRA. Unhand me!

Robert pretends to release Sandra's hand.

Oh Charles! One last embrace!

ROBERT. I cannot bear to see my sister in such grief!

SANDRA. Who could do such a thing! The night of our engagement party! Cecil! Quick! Your brother's dead!

DENNIS. *(Off.)* This way Master Haversham!

MAX. *(Off.)* I'm coming Miss Colleymoore!

Max enters through the door without difficulty, followed by Dennis.

Brother? Dead! It can't be!

ROBERT. Calm yourself Cecil. Pour him a stiff drink, Perkins.

DENNIS. Right away sir!

Dennis produces a full bottle of scotch.

Oh my god! He's drunk the whole bottle sir! There's not a drop left!

Dennis tries to get rid of the scotch, pouring it quietly into the coal scuttle.

There's not a drop left!

ROBERT. Hang it all! There's another on the shelf!

DENNIS. Of course sir! Yes, this one is full!

Dennis produces the empty bottle he should have got the first time.

ROBERT. This is horrifying! I mean who on earth would have a motivation to murder Charles Haversham?

Dennis puts the empty bottle onto a tray along with a glass and walks past the window. As he passes the window, Annie leans through and exchanges the empty bottle for a full plastic bottle of white spirit with a large flammable symbol on it. Dennis doesn't see the switch, but then sees the fresh bottle and is baffled by this.

SANDRA. I can't imagine!

Dennis hands a glass to Max.

MAX. Thank you, Perkins.

Dennis pours the "scotch" into Max's glass.

ROBERT. It's unthinkable! Right here in his own private rooms at Haversham Manor.

SANDRA. It's terrible! Just a week after our engagement!

MAX. He was a good brother.

Max drinks the white spirit. He suddenly spits it back out.

That's the best whisky I've ever tasted!

ROBERT. Have another, to calm your nerves.

MAX. Thank you, Perkins.

ROBERT. Make it a double!

Dennis pours another glass of white spirit. Max drinks it again. It is horrible again.

SANDRA. Oh! My Charles! My Charles! My head is spinning! I'm going to become hysterical!

ROBERT. Calm down, Florence.

DENNIS. Another whisky, sir?

MAX. *Yes!*

SANDRA. I can't believe Charles was sat up here alone, drinking, when he was supposed to be downstairs with us.

MAX. My brother wasn't as happy as he led people to believe. Underneath that cheerful mask lay a darker side to the man that many didn't know about.

DENNIS. It's true, his smile was often just a *(Reads from his hand.)* façade. I was fortunate enough to be one of the only people he truly confided in. I've lost a real friend today.

ROBERT. We all have, Perkins. Hang it, I knew Charles ever since school.

SANDRA. I don't know how I'll ever recover from this.

ROBERT. You'll move back home with me. I'm your brother and I'll have it no other way.

MAX. Perkins is right, my brother was hiding a deep sense of melancholy and resentment. There's no doubt in my mind, it was suicide.

ROBERT. Suicide Cecil? How can you say that! Of course not; it's murder! Murder in the first degree!

MAX. Nonsense, the man was paranoid, jealous, and I can prove it! Perkins, hand me his journal from the mantelpiece!

Annie's hand pops through the curtains, holding a journal in position. Dennis passes it to Max.

Why, look at the last entry. *(Not looking at the journal.) "I fear Florence does not love me. The night of our engagement party; despair engulfs my soul."*

SANDRA. But I love Charles with all my heart!

Max returns the journal to the missing mantelpiece; it falls straight to the floor.

MAX. As I said! Driven mad with paranoia and jealousy.

All gasp and suddenly face out. Silence. The cast wait for a sound effect that doesn't happen. Eventually a loud door chime sounds, late.

ALL. *(React.)* The Inspector!

SANDRA. Thank heavens he's here!

Chris (playing Inspector Carter) enters through the door, covered in paper snowflakes, carrying an attaché case.

CHRIS. What a terrible snowstorm. Good evening, I'm Inspector Carter. Take my case.

DENNIS. Yes, Inspector.

Chris hands his case to Dennis, who places it on the floor by the table.

CHRIS. This must be Charles Haversham! I'm sorry; this must've given you all a *damn* shock.

SANDRA. *(Smiling.)* It did, we're all still reeling!

CHRIS. Naturally. Are any of you the deceased's immediate family?

MAX. I'm Cecil Haversham. I'm his brother.

SANDRA. I'm Florence Colleymoore. I'm his fiancée. Tonight was our engagement party.

CHRIS. What a damn, *sad* thing. You! Have you poured everyone a stiff drink?

DENNIS. Yes, Inspector.

Dennis holds out the tray and all take a glass. Dennis removes the tray, knocking Jonathan on the head.

MAX. Let us raise a glass: the man we all loved. To Charles!

ALL. Charles!

All drink the white spirit. They all gag, spit it out and recover.

CHRIS. Delicious.

SANDRA. Excellent.

ROBERT. Lovely.

CHRIS. Listen, you all must be distraught, but forgive me, the sooner I can begin my enquiries, the sooner we can all get to the bottom of this ghastly business.

Chris deposits the Inspector's notebook on the table.

(To Dennis.) If you'd be so kind as to bring the body downstairs, so I can examine it.

DENNIS. Yes, Inspector.

ROBERT. I'll lend you a hand, Perkins.

CHRIS. Then lock all the doors to the house and prepare this room, I'll conduct my enquiries in here afterwards.

DENNIS. Inspector.

Over the next few lines, Dennis brings in a stretcher. Robert and Dennis try to lift Jonathan onto the stretcher but can't. They roll him off of the chaise longue onto the floor. They then go to lift the stretcher up, the canvas tears off of the stretcher, and Robert and Dennis are left holding just the poles. Confused about what to do, they carry just the poles off through the door.

MAX. Any ideas on the cause of death, Inspector?

CHRIS. Could be a number of things. Suffocation, strangulation, poison. Before fully examining the body I wouldn't like to say.

SANDRA. How *could* someone do it?!

CHRIS. Try not to think about it, Miss Colleymoore. Once I've finished downstairs I'll speak to you each individually and then perhaps you can get some space to calm your nerves.

SANDRA. Thank you Inspector, this is all more than I can bear.

CHRIS. I'll be back presently, as soon as I've finished examining the body.

Chris exits, shutting the door behind him. Jonathan has realised that he is meant to have been carried off and slowly starts to get up, trying not to be seen, and exits towards the door, dragging the stretcher canvas with him. Sandra and Max stare at Jonathan as he slowly leaves through the door and shuts it behind him, getting the stretcher canvas caught in the door. Jonathan pulls the canvas through the crack in the door, the last bit of it gets stuck; he tugs at it, causing the door to swing open, revealing him. Sandra closes the door.

MAX. Thank God they've all gone!

SANDRA. Don't say a word! If they find out about us, we'll be suspects!

MAX. You and I were having an affair, what of it? It doesn't mean we killed him.

SANDRA. Of course not! But that's what the Inspector will think!

MAX. It's fine, we'll just carry on as if everything's just as it was.

Max sits on the chaise longue and discovers a ledger under the cushions. In confusion he moves it under the chaise longue.

Except now you won't be forced to marry my beastly brother.

SANDRA. And soon, we can be together and not keep secrets.

MAX. But please, while we're here, just the two of us, let me steal one quick kiss!

SANDRA. Cecil, we can't! If we're caught it would be the end!

MAX. I can't resist you Florence! I can't control myself!

Robert bursts in.

ROBERT. The Inspector requires a pencil! What on earth's going on in here?

SANDRA. Sorry, I felt flustered! Cecil was cooling my brow!

MAX. Just cooling her brow.

ROBERT. I don't see how my sister's brow is any business of yours, Haversham!

SANDRA. Don't be a prig Tom, Cecil was only trying to help.

MAX. Yes, *Tom.*

ROBERT. Very well, if you'll excuse me, I have the *pencil.*

Robert sees that there is no pencil. In a panic he grabs the set of keys. Robert exits, closing the door.

MAX. Thank God he's gone! That man's such a nuisance!

SANDRA. He is my brother!

MAX. Let me kiss you! Just once!

SANDRA. Oh, Cecil! Kiss me a thousand times! I'm yours!

Dennis bursts in.

DENNIS. Sorry to disturb you Miss Colleymoore, Mr. Haversham, I've come to collect the keys to lock us all inside.

MAX. They're by the telephone, Perkins.

Dennis cannot see the keys; instead he takes the Inspector's notebook.

DENNIS. I shall lock the doors at once.

Dennis exits with the Inspector's notebook.

SANDRA. You don't think Perkins suspects us, do you?

MAX. That old fool, of course not.

SANDRA. Oh Cecil! My passion makes me forget myself!

Robert bursts in.

ROBERT. I forgot the Inspector's notepad… what in God's name!

SANDRA. I was about to faint! Cecil caught me!

ROBERT. You know Cecil; I don't appreciate you trying to get your hands on my sister on the night of her fiancé's death.

MAX. You ought to take better care of her then, Colleymoore.

SANDRA. I'm overcome!

ROBERT. I haven't time for this! Now I have the *Inspector's notebook,* I'll be on my way.

The notebook is nowhere to be seen. Robert takes the vase instead and exits.

MAX. Blasted interruptions!

SANDRA. Kiss me Cecil!

MAX. I want you Florence! You make my heart beat out of my chest!

SANDRA. Your eyes send me into a dream! Kiss me Cecil, I can't wait a second longer!

Pause. Dennis is supposed to have burst in. They look at the door. Vamp. Until eventually Dennis bursts in, late, holding two candlesticks.

DENNIS. Sorry to interrupt again Mr. Haversham, Miss Colleymoore. I've just come to prepare the room.

MAX. Thank you Perkins. Put them on the mantelpiece.

Dennis walks to the mantelpiece with the candlesticks. He goes to put them down and Annie leans through the window and holds the mantelpiece in position. Dennis exits and Annie remains, staring at the others.

At last we're alone.

Annie stares awkwardly from the window.

SANDRA. Oh Cecil! Let's run away from here! Far away! Together!

MAX. Soon, my love, but we must be careful. We mustn't arouse suspicion.

SANDRA. Cecil, tell me, who do you think killed Charles!

MAX. There's no question in my mind Florence, he was killed by your brother, Thomas Colleymoore!

SANDRA. My brother! What a devil of a situation this is!

Jonathan suddenly bursts through the door holding a pistol.

JONATHAN. *Not so fast, Inspector!!*

Max and Sandra stare at Jonathan, who realises he has come in much too early and hurriedly exits.

SANDRA. But, why would Thomas want Charles dead?

MAX. Isn't it obvious? He was always bitter and possessive when it came to you! He didn't like the idea of his best friend marrying his sister. He saw you together at tonight's engagement party and it drove him half mad and he snapped and killed Charles!

SANDRA. But, if it is Thomas, what if he finds out about you and I?

MAX. I don't think there's any doubt. He would try and kill us, just like he killed Charles!

SANDRA. Oh, I feel faint again!

MAX. Don't worry Florence! Just follow my lead…

Chris enters.

CHRIS. I'm sorry to have kept you, but now I have inspected the body more closely, our interview can proceed. *(Calls through the door.)* Perkins! Bring in Charles' personal effects.

Dennis enters with several props, including a letter.

DENNIS. Where would you like them, Inspector?

CHRIS. Set them down on the mantelpiece.

DENNIS. As you wish, Inspector.

Chris realises what he's said. Dennis carries the props over to Annie, who is still holding up the mantelpiece. Dennis hands her all of the items carefully. Annie struggles under the weight of the mantelpiece throughout the next exchange.

Silence. Dennis is supposed to leave but doesn't.

CHRIS. Don't go, Perkins,

Dennis goes to leave and then stops. He sits down on the chaise longue.

I'd like to ask you a few questions first. Mr. Haversham, Miss Colleymoore, perhaps you'd be so kind as to give us a moment's privacy.

MAX. Naturally.

Max and Sandra exit.

CHRIS. Don't just stand there, Perkins. Take a seat.

Dennis remains sat.

I don't smoke.

Dennis offers his cigarette case to Chris.

But you go ahead. How are you feeling, Perkins?

DENNIS. A little shaken sir, but I'll be fine.

Dennis goes to light himself a cigarette; he burns his hand and drops the match into the coal scuttle, where it ignites the scotch. Annie is alarmed by the fire and drops all of the props loudly onto the floor. Terrified, she moves out of sight behind the flats.

CHRIS. You were close with Charles Haversham?

DENNIS. Yes, sir, very close.

CHRIS. You don't appear very upset by his death.

DENNIS. On the *(Hand check.)* contrary, I've barely taken it in. Oh, he was such a kindly, charming man.

CHRIS. It's true.

DENNIS. You met him?

CHRIS. Once, briefly at the local police station, he…

Robert leans through the window with a fire extinguisher and puts out the fire. Robert realises he's been seen.

ROBERT. *(Ad-libs.)* Evening, Inspector. *(Withdraws.)*

CHRIS. Once, briefly at the local police station, he…

ROBERT. *(Off.)* Of course they didn't notice.

CHRIS. …police station, he came in…

ROBERT. *(Off.)* I ad-libbed.

CHRIS. He came in as a consultant on a fraud case I was working on.

DENNIS. I see.

CHRIS. How long have you been working at Haversham Manor?

DENNIS. Eighty years.

CHRIS. Eighty / years?

DENNIS. *(Corrects himself.)* Eight years.

CHRIS. Eight years. And have you enjoyed your time here?

DENNIS. My time with Mr. Haversham has been a joy, I feel that since I've come here I have been seen not only as a butler but also as a friend, a confidant; if you need me again I'll be in my quarters, exits.

CHRIS. *Exits.*

DENNIS. Exits.

Silence. Dennis realises and turns to go.

CHRIS. If you'd be so kind as to send in Florence Colleymoore on your way out.

Sandra bursts in, followed by Robert. Dennis exits.

SANDRA. No need, I'm already here! Don't ask too much of me Inspector, I feel fragile as glass.

ROBERT. Don't harass her Carter; she's been through a lot tonight.

CHRIS. At last Colleymoore, you found me a pencil?

ROBERT. Yes, Inspector.

Robert hands Chris the keys.

CHRIS. Thank you, and my notebook?

Robert hands Chris the vase.

I knew I'd left them somewhere. Now I must to speak to Miss Colleymoore alone.

ROBERT. Very well. I'll be in the library, Florence.

Robert exits. Chris questions Sandra, making notes with the keys and vase.

CHRIS. Don't fret Miss Colleymoore, my questions will be brief and to the point and then you can get some rest. Firstly, how old are you Miss Colleymore?

SANDRA. Twenty-one.

CHRIS. I'll make a note of that.

He tries to make a note on the vase.

How long ago did you first meet your fiancé?

SANDRA. Only seven months ago. But my brother has known him years.

Chris writes on vase again.

CHRIS. When were you due to be married?

SANDRA. In the new year.

CHRIS. Well, that's enough notes for now, I think Miss Colleymoore. Did y…

Sandra comes in a line too early.

SANDRA. When you love someone there's *no such thing* as rushing, Inspector.

CHRIS. Did you ever think you were rushing into this marriage?

SANDRA. Why wouldn't I love him?

CHRIS. ...did you love him, then?

SANDRA. *How could anyone have benefitted?*

CHRIS. Can you think of anyone who might have benefitted from your fiancé's death?

SANDRA. *Cecil?!*

CHRIS. Not even *Cecil*?

SANDRA. *(Slaps Chris.)* Don't tell me to calm down!

CHRIS. Calm down Miss Colleymoore. *(Reacts to slap.)*

SANDRA. I wasn't having an affair! Don't raise your voice to me, Inspector!

CHRIS. YOU WERE HAVING AN AFFAIR!

SANDRA. *What* letter?

CHRIS. Then, how do you explain the letter on the mantelpiece?

SANDRA. I *didn't* write that letter!

CHRIS. You wrote that *letter*!

Annie has taken the letter offstage and she passes it back through the window.

SANDRA. You've read my letter? Where did you find it?

CHRIS. Addressed to Cecil, written in your hand, declaring your love for him and how the thought of marrying Charles repulsed you.

SANDRA. Charles read it...

CHRIS. *(Does Sandra's line for her.)* You've read my letter? Where did you find it? *(His own line.)* In Charles' pocket!

SANDRA. Charles read it?! Then it *was* suicide!

CHRIS. Or a murder, conceived by you and Cecil Haversham so you could run away together!

SANDRA. How could you even say such a thing! It's true; Cecil and I were having an affair! We loved each other! But that's all; neither of us wanted to hurt Charles, let alone kill him.

CHRIS. It's my job to ask difficult questions Miss Colleymoore, I'm sorry if this upsets you.

SANDRA. *Upsets me?* How dare you! My fiancé was murdered in this very room, a matter of hours ago! I find your manner most unbefitting! I shall make a formal complaint to Scotland Yard.

CHRIS. Scotland Yard will not listen to the complaints of a murderess!

SANDRA. You diabolical beast! How can you? I won't stand for this, Inspector! Accuse me again and you'll be sor…

Robert bursts in, followed by Max; the door hits Sandra sharply on the head and she collapses, unconscious.

ROBERT. What's all this shouting!

MAX. What is this, Inspector?

All register that Sandra is on the floor.

CHRIS. I'm merely interviewing Miss Colleymoore, nothing more.

MAX. Florence, calm down, stop shouting!

Sandra remains unconscious.

ROBERT. She's having one of her episodes. Snap out of it, you're hysterical!

Sandra remains unconscious.

MAX. Florence! Where are you going?

Sandra remains unconscious.

ROBERT. Come back here this instant!

Sandra remains unconscious.

She's run off. I'll fetch her back. You stay here Cecil, I daresay the Inspector has some questions for you; you were Charles' brother after all.

Robert exits.

MAX. I'm sorry, Inspector, she's badly shaken, we all are. It's been quite a night and it's getting late.

CHRIS. *(Looks at clock.)* Eleven o'clock already.

The clock says 5:30.

MAX. Well Inspector? Do you have any questions for me?

Robert peers through the curtains to see if Sandra is alright.

CHRIS. Oh yes Mr. Haversham, similar questions to those I asked Miss Colleymoore.

MAX. Fire away Inspector, I'm at your service.

CHRIS. Indeed, you and your brother, did you get along well?

MAX. Up and down. Since Father died there was rather more strain on our relationship; it was no secret our father cared for Charles more than myself.

CHRIS. This is your father in the portrait, is it not?

It's a painting of a dog.

MAX. It is.

CHRIS. He looks the spit of Charles, doesn't he?

MAX. He did ever since he was quite young.

CHRIS. You were the junior by four years?

MAX. Almost four, yes…

Robert, Jonathan and Annie peer through the curtain together to see if Sandra is alright.

And didn't I know it, Charles patronised and embarrassed me throughout our childhood. He always thought he knew best, and Father always took his side. If he ever didn't get his way, he was unbearable.

Now Annie, Robert and Jonathan all reach through the window and start to lift Sandra out under the curtains.

CHRIS. He sounds far from the ideal brother. It sounds like you hated one another.

MAX. I won't lie Inspector, Charles and I never truly saw eye to eye, but if you're suggesting I had something to do with his death, you're mistaken.

CHRIS. I see. It's a dark night, Cecil.

Chris pulls the curtains open, revealing Robert, Annie and Jonathan. They all freeze and try not to be seen. Sandra is held unconscious, in an awkward position.

MAX. Inspector?

CHRIS. You can barely even make out the trees.

MAX. What are you saying, Inspector?

CHRIS. I'm saying, Cecil, that tonight would be the perfect night for you to murder your brother.

Chris and Max turn back downstage. Robert, Annie and Jonathan continue to remove Sandra.

MAX. Inspector, please, me and my brother had our differences, but deep down we cared for one another…

CHRIS. *(Offhand.)* And yet you had an affair with his fiancée?

Robert, Annie and Jonathan drop Sandra and start again.

MAX. …What on earth gave you that idea?

CHRIS. The letter I found in Charles' pocket from Miss Colleymoore to yourself.

MAX. *(Shaken.)* You know about that?

CHRIS. As, it seems, did Charles.

Robert, Annie and Jonathan have managed to get Sandra out of the window. Annie pulls the curtains shut.

MAX. Well… Bravo Inspector! Very good. You've found out about Florence and I, but it proves nothing. We didn't have a thing to do with Charles' murder, but I *can* tell you who does.

CHRIS. Who?

MAX. Thomas Colleymoore.

CHRIS. Colleymoore? But he and Charles were old friends, were they not?

MAX. He's a dangerously unhinged man, with a devil of a temper and Florence is his sister. I've said it before and I shall say it again: he couldn't give his sister up to any man, much less his old school chum. Tonight's engagement party made him lose control and he lashed out at Charles. A crime of passion perhaps, but there it is.

CHRIS. Thank you Mr. Haversham, you've been most helpful. Perhaps you could fetch Thomas Colleymoore. I'm going to need to follow more than one line of enquiry at a time to get to the bottom of this.

MAX. At once, Inspector, anything to help the progress of your investigation.

Max exits.

CHRIS. Hang it all Charles. Who could've killed you? Everybody under this damned roof seems guilty.

Chris sits on the chaise longue.

That's queer. There's something underneath these cushions. A ledger?

Chris removes the cushions from the chaise longue; there is no ledger. He begins to search for it, pulling off the chaise longue's lining, looking inside the pillows. Vamps to cover. Eventually finds it underneath the chaise longue itself.

A ledger! With Charles' initials inscribed on the cover. What's inside? Notes…bills…what's this? The Last Will and Testament of Charles Haversham…dated only today?…

Chris tries to take the ribbon off of the document, but he can't; he reads off of the closed document.

Let me see… *"I Charles Haversham, hereby amend my last will and testament to leave my money, Haversham Manor and all its contents and grounds to one…"* Good Lord!

Max and Robert enter. Chris hurriedly puts the ledger and paper away.

MAX. Thomas Colleymoore for you Inspector.

CHRIS. Ah, thank you Cecil. Tell me, did Charles have a study where he kept his papers?

MAX. Of course, second door on the right.

CHRIS. I'll return presently.

MAX. Take your time, Inspector.

ROBERT. Indeed.

Chris hurriedly exits.

MAX. Did you find Florence?

ROBERT. She ran out into the grounds.

Robert shuts the door after Chris, causing the clock to fall off the wall. Robert picks up the clock and puts it back on the wall, knocking the barometer off. Max picks up the barometer and puts it back on the wall, causing the painting to fall down. Max goes to hold up the painting, leaving the barometer to Robert. They are left holding all three items up.

MAX. Tell me Thomas, what were your feelings about Charles and Florence's engagement?

ROBERT. I was overjoyed of course. I love Florence and I loved Charles, I couldn't have approved more of the match.

MAX. But Colleymoore, it's well known that you're protective of your sister.

The telephone rings.

I'll get it.

Max tries hard to keep holding the picture against the wall and reach for the phone; it takes him a while. The phone keeps ringing; eventually he manages to pick up the receiver.

Good evening. *(Beat.)* It's for you.

ROBERT. Who the devil is it?

MAX. Your accountants, Colleymoore.

ROBERT. At eleven thirty in the evening?

MAX. Yes.

Max tries painfully to pass the receiver to Robert. Robert eventually gets it, keeping the clock and barometer on the wall using his head.

ROBERT. *(Speaking in extreme discomfort.)* Good evening. Yes, Thomas Colleymoore speaking. It *is inconvenient, yes!* ...My recent deposits? What of them? ...Discrepancies? What are you talking about man? ...*Gone?* Gone where? ...Nine thousand pounds *stolen*! Good God man! Perkins, get in here.

Dennis enters through the door as far as he can.

DENNIS. Yes, sir.

ROBERT. Perkins, fetch me my bankbook.

Dennis passes Robert the bankbook.

DENNIS. Your bankbook, sir.

Dennis puts the bankbook into Robert's mouth. Then Dennis passes a pen through the door and puts this in Robert's mouth as well.

ROBERT. Thank you, Perkins.

Robert rearranges himself to take the phone again.

How could you allow this to happen? This is an absolute disgrace! I shall report you to your superiors. Who am I speaking with? Mr. Fitzroy. I'll write that name down.

Robert writes the name in his bankbook with a lot of difficulty.

Fi…tz…roy, I'll have you know this telephone call has put me in a very difficult position. I shall hang up the phone this instant!

Robert throws the phone to Max, who hangs it up.

MAX. What is it, Colleymoore?

ROBERT. Money, stolen from my accounts!

MAX. Good lord!

ROBERT. Nine thousand pounds stolen from my private savings.

MAX. Most irregular!

ROBERT. What a ghastly business. First my oldest friend murdered in cold blood and now I find myself on the edge of financial ruin! This evening could get no worse!

MAX. Thomas, I have a confession. I wasn't going to say anything, but well, the Inspector seems to have found out and blast it, I'm tired of keeping secrets.

ROBERT. Spit it out, Cecil.

MAX. Well… Florence and I are having an affair!

ROBERT. *WHAT?!*

Robert launches himself at Max, who dives downstage. The portrait, clock and barometer mysteriously all stay hung in their positions. Robert and Max double-take.

You and my sister?!

Robert throws Max over the chaise longue.

MAX. Now, calm down, Colleymoore.

ROBERT. I knew it! You always were a snake in the grass.

Robert drags Max up by his hair, accidentally slamming him into the side of the set.

MAX. It's not what you think! We're in love!

ROBERT. My sister does not love you. How dare you lay a finger on her; your own brother's fiancée! It's disgusting! No wonder your father hated you!

Robert opens the door to throw Max outside. Dennis is stood waiting for his entrance and shuts the door. Robert, not seeing this, throws Max into the door.

MAX. *(Dazed.)* Don't speak about my father that way, Colleymoore!

ROBERT. Well, it seems there's no doubt about who killed Charles anymore. He was killed by his own vile little brother in a fit of jealous rage.

Robert helps Max offstage.

MAX. I shan't stand for this, Colleymoore!

ROBERT. You'll be sorry you ever laid a finger on my sister, Haversham. You'll be sorry!

Robert slams the door, hitting Max in the face one last time. The portrait, clock, barometer and curtain rail all fall off the wall, revealing Dennis in the window with a glass of water on a tray. He hurriedly enters through the door and sets the tray down by the telephone. Suddenly three loud gunshots and a scream are heard offstage.

(Off.) Gunshots in the library!

DENNIS. By Jove!

Chris rushes in.

CHRIS. Dear God, what's going on?

DENNIS. I don't know Inspector, I was in here when I heard screams from downstairs!

Robert enters, calling off.

ROBERT. Get in here now Florence! It's not safe down there!

Robert drags Annie in through the door; she's wearing Sandra's dress over her own clothes and she clutches a script.

ANNIE. *(Reads each word slowly from the script in an American accent.)* Thomas I'm frightened!

ROBERT. Don't worry Florence, you're safe in here.

DENNIS. What's going on?

CHRIS. Isn't it obvious! Cecil has lost control!

ANNIE. Cecil! Surely not!

CHRIS. He killed Charles tonight, driven mad by his lust for you, and now he knows we've found him out!

ANNIE. I cannot bear it. Cecil would not do such a thing.

ROBERT. Of course he would, the damn lunatic!

ANNIE. You used to trust people Tom; you've changed!

DENNIS. This is a fine mess, sir! The worst night I've seen in eighty—eight years of service!

ANNIE. Save me brother, save me!

She clings on to Chris. Chris pushes her onto Robert.

ROBERT. I shan't let anyone hurt a hair on your head, Florence.

ANNIE. I'm panicking! I can't believe…Cecil?

CHRIS. *Cecil!*

ANNIE. Cecil…is doing this.

DENNIS. Try to stay calm Miss Colleymoore!

ANNIE. I shall faint!

Annie falls back without warning; Robert just catches her.

ROBERT. You shan't faint, confound it! What a devil of a situation this is!

Jonathan bursts in again, holding his pistol.

JONATHAN. Not so fast Inspector!

Jonathan realises he is still too early, and exits again. After leaving he slowly walks past the window, his head in his hands. He realises the audience can see him; mortified, he darts out of view.

ROBERT. We're all going to survive tonight, you hear me?

Chris peers out of the door. Shouting gets louder outside.

CHRIS. Take cover!

ROBERT. Great Scot!

DENNIS. *Good heavens!*

ANNIE. Ay, me!

CHRIS. Don't panic! Cecil's crossing the landing.

ANNIE. We must lock him out!

ROBERT. Where are the keys to the door Perkins?

DENNIS. Here they are, sir!

Dennis pulls out the notebook from his pocket. Chris throws the vase to Dennis, the keys fly out, Dennis catches them.

Here they are, sir!

CHRIS. Quickly Perkins, hand them to me before Cecil…

The door bursts open and Max staggers inside. He shuffles forward a few paces and then flops dead onto the chaise longue. Three bullet wounds in his back.

Good lord!

Short musical spike.

ANNIE. Cecil's dead?

Same short musical spike. Chris checks Max's pulse.

DENNIS. A double murder!

A short snatch of an English new wave song like "Girls on Film" by Duran Duran plays, then suddenly the correct musical spike cuts in.*

TREVOR. *(From box.)* Found the Duran Duran**, carry on.

CHRIS. Time of death: quarter to midnight.

He checks where the clock used to be.

ANNIE. *(With genuine affection.)* Cecil! No! No! No! I loved him! I *loved* him! I know it's wrong. I know I was engaged to Charles; but Cecil was mine *and.*

Silence. Chris turns the page in her script.

…*I* was his. I loved him!

DENNIS. There, there, Miss Colleymoore.

ANNIE. Through tears. How will I go on?

ROBERT. But who could've killed him?

DENNIS. That's a good question Mr. Colleymoore.

* See Note on Songs/Recordings at the back of this volume.

** If a song by a different band is used, change "Duran Duran" appropriately.

CHRIS. …and one we need to answer quickly if we all want to get out of this house alive.

ANNIE. Oh Inspector, you've given me a chill!

CHRIS. Perkins, pour us all another scotch.

DENNIS. Of course, Inspector.

Dennis pours more white spirit for everyone.

CHRIS. Now, tell me, is there anyone you know of still in the grounds other than the four of us?

ANNIE. Not a soul.

ROBERT. The staff all go home at the weekends, except for Perkins of course. *(Drinks and spits out the white spirit.)* Good God, I needed that.

CHRIS. Does anyone else have access to the grounds?

ANNIE. No one, Inspector.

DENNIS. I'm the only one with the master key and as instructed I locked and bolted the doors as soon as you arrived.

ROBERT. Then who could have killed him?

The script goes round in a loop.

DENNIS. That's a good question Mr. Colleymoore.

CHRIS. …and one we need to answer quickly if we all want to get out of this house alive.

ANNIE. Inspector, you've given me a chill!

CHRIS. Perkins, pour us all another scotch.

DENNIS. Of course, Inspector.

Dennis pours white spirit again.

CHRIS. Now, tell me, is there anyone who you know of still in the grounds other than the four of us?

ANNIE. Not a soul.

ROBERT. The staff all go home at the weekends, except for Perkins of course. *(Drinks. Spits out again.)* Good God, I needed that.

CHRIS. Does anyone have access to the grounds?

ANNIE. No one, Inspector.

DENNIS. I'm the only one with the master key and as instructed I locked and bolted the doors as soon as you arrived.

ROBERT. Then who could've killed him?

Dennis doesn't realise and the loop goes around again.

DENNIS. That's a good question Mr. Colleymoore.

CHRIS. …and one we need to answer *quickly* if we all want to get out of this house alive.

ANNIE. Inspector, you've given me a chill!

CHRIS. Perkins, pour us all another scotch.

DENNIS. Of course, Inspector.

Dennis pours white spirit again.

CHRIS. Now, tell me, is there anyone who you know of still in the grounds other than the four of us?

ANNIE. Not a soul.

ROBERT. The staff all go home at the weekends, except for Perkins of course. *(Drinks.)* Good God, I needed that.

CHRIS. Does anyone have access to the grounds?

ANNIE. No one, Inspector.

DENNIS. I'm the only one with the master key and as instructed I locked and bolted all the doors as soon as you arrived.

ROBERT. Then who could've killed him?

Script loops again.

DENNIS. That's a good question Mr. Colleymoore.

CHRIS. …and one we need to answer quickly if we all want to get out of this house alive.

ANNIE. Inspector, you've given me a chill!

CHRIS. Perkins, pour us all another scotch.

DENNIS. Of course, Inspector.

Dennis pours white spirit again.

CHRIS. Now, tell me, is there anyone who you know of still in the grounds other than the four of us?

ANNIE. Not a soul.

ROBERT. The staff all go home at the weekends, except for Perkins of course. *(Drinks again. Spits out again.)* Good God, I needed that.

CHRIS. Does anyone have access to the grounds?

ANNIE. No one, Inspector.

DENNIS. I'm the only one with the master key and as instructed I locked and bolted the doors as soon as you arrived.

ROBERT. Then who could've killed him?

Script loops again.

DENNIS. That's a good question Mr. Colleymoore.

CHRIS. …and one we need to answer quickly if we all want to get out of this house alive.

ANNIE. Inspector, you've given me a chill!

CHRIS. Perkins, pour us all another scotch.

DENNIS. Of course, Inspector.

Dennis pours white spirit again.

CHRIS. Now, tell me, is there anyone who you know of still in the grounds other than the four of us?

ANNIE. Not a soul.

ROBERT. The staff all go home at the weekends, except for Perkins of course. *(Throws the white spirit over Dennis.)* Good God, I needed that.

CHRIS. Does anyone have access to the grounds?

ANNIE. No one, Inspector.

DENNIS. I'm the only one with the master key and as instructed I locked and bolted all the doors as soon as you arrived.

ROBERT. Then who could've killed him?

DENNIS. *(Realises.)* No one could have killed him! Except the people in this room.

All gasp.

ROBERT. You're right, it's one of us!

CHRIS. Hang it all! I'm stuck in a room full of murderers!

He drinks his glass and spits it out over Max.

DENNIS. Damn and blast!

CHRIS. One of you killed Charles and Cecil Haversham and we shan't leave the house until the matter is solved. You! Take this body outside!

DENNIS. Yes, sir!

ROBERT. I'll lend you a hand, Perkins.

Dennis opens the door and pulls out the two stretcher poles from earlier. Dennis and Robert lay them on the floor before rolling Max on top of the two poles. They lift the poles, optimistically. Max grasps them and holding on for dear life they carry him towards the door. Robert and Dennis can't get Max off through the door, so tip him onto his side and exit through the door and past the window.

CHRIS. So, let us go over the facts.

ANNIE. *(Goes to window.)* Oh! It's such a terrible night!

CHRIS. Florence! You were engaged to be married to Charles, a man who according to your letter you despised. Not only this but you were having an affair with his brother—

ANNIE. *Cecil!*

CHRIS. ...Cecil. It seems plausible to me that you both murdered him so you could be together.

ANNIE. Oh! Stop it Inspector! Cecil's dead too now and I certainly didn't kill Ch...

Robert bursts back in, knocking Annie out with the door.

ROBERT. What's going on, Ins...

CHRIS. You're lying, Florence! You killed him!

Annie remains unconscious.

ROBERT. *(Helpless.)* She's having another of her hysterical episodes.

Annie remains unconscious.

DENNIS. Try to relax, Miss Colleymoore!

ROBERT. Florence, behave with some decorum! Remember yourself!

DENNIS. Someone ought to fetch her medication!

ROBERT. I'll go.

Robert goes to the door. It doesn't open.

Someone's locked the door! Good God. We're trapped.

The door comes off in Robert's hand.

CHRIS. Trapped! My God!

Robert drags the door offstage.

You killed your fiancé, Florence! What do you have to say for yourself?

All look to Annie's unconscious form. Desperately waiting for her line. Eventually Robert tries to cover his mouth and do Florence's line.

ROBERT. *(High voice.)* I am an honourable woman, Inspector.

CHRIS. You're lying, Florence! You killed him!

ROBERT. *(High voice.)* I won't stand another second of this, Inspector! You're all beasts!

CHRIS. Did you enjoy killing your husband, Miss Colleymore?

ROBERT. *(High voice.)* How dare you make such an accusation Inspector! *(Normal voice.)* Calm down, Florence! Really! *(High voice.)* I can't stand another minute in this room. If I can't get out of the door I shall descend from the window.

CHRIS. Oh my god! She's trying to climb out of the window.

All rush to Annie and pick her up and try and push her out of the window. Vamp to cover. Sandra enters through the door in her underwear, unseen by the others. Eventually she comes in with her line.

SANDRA. I am no murderer!

All turn to face Sandra, leaving Annie wedged in the window.

CHRIS. Calm yourself, Miss Colleymoore. You and Cecil both have *plausible* motives for murder…but not the *true* motive!

SANDRA. What are you saying, Inspector?

CHRIS. I'm saying the *true* motive belongs to Perkins!

Annie becomes dislodged from the window and falls to the floor.

SANDRA. Perkins?

DENNIS. Me, Inspector?

CHRIS. You Perkins! A little earlier I stumbled across Charles' newly written last will and testament, dated only today, declaring that Charles wanted to make Perkins the sole beneficiary of his inheritance.

Sandra grabs the dress.

SANDRA. Surely not Perkins!

DENNIS. This is all a mistake!

CHRIS. Save your pleading for the police station. Cuff him Thomas.

He throws handcuffs to Robert, who cuffs Dennis to the chaise longue.

I'll drive you there myself as soon as the snowstorm has passed.

SANDRA. That won't be for hours, the snow is at its peak!

Max throws a clump of snow in from the window.

DENNIS. It's not true, I tell you!

SANDRA. Surely...Perkins didn't kill Cecil as well?

ROBERT. Of course he did. Cecil found him out and Perkins killed him to keep him quiet.

DENNIS. There must be some misunderstanding! I haven't killed anyone. But I know who has!

ROBERT. You know who killed Charles?

DENNIS. I do!

ALL. Who?!

DENNIS. *THE INSPECTOR DID!*

All gasp.

ROBERT. What on earth?

CHRIS. Poppycock!

DENNIS. You did! And I know why!

CHRIS. Shut your mouth, Perkins!

DENNIS. You did it because Charles knew about the police money you were *(Checks hand.)* embezzling.

CHRIS. Nonsense!

DENNIS. You mentioned you had several *(Checks hand.)* rendezvous with Charles before, at the local police station. You said he was a consultant on a fraud case you were working on.

ROBERT. What of it?

DENNIS. Charles came home that evening very intrigued by the whole case. He decided to look into the matter personally. He found the reason why no arrests had been made were because the man committing the fraud was yourself. You were the *(Checks hand.)* embezzling. *(Checks other hand.)* The perpetrator! You were the perpetrator!

CHRIS. You can't prove it!

DENNIS. But Charles *could* and that's why you killed him!

CHRIS. Never!

DENNIS. I know your secret, Inspector! What will you do? Kill me too?

Chris draws a gun and points it at Dennis.

CHRIS. I will! Confound it!

SANDRA. What a devil of a situation this is!

Jonathan enters again, holding his gun.

JONATHAN. *Not so fast Inspector!*

All hugely shocked at this.

ROBERT. Charles?

CHRIS. Mr. Haversham?

SANDRA. Charley! I thought you were dead!

CHRIS. You're alive? It's not possible.

JONATHAN. Oh, I'm afraid it is. You couldn't kill me that ea…

Loud, long dramatic musical spike is played again, late.

…easily.

CHRIS. How did you survive?

JONATHAN. I simply didn't drink the poisoned water you left out for me this afternoon!

CHRIS. *(To Dennis.)* How did you know it was me?!

JONATHAN. *I* told Perkins! We've been working together all along. Ever since we last spoke at the police station it was clear you thought I was onto you. It was at this point I became afraid you'd try to kill me. For months now I've had my guard up and tonight you fell into my trap.

DENNIS. You've been hiding in the grounds ever since this afternoon when you planted the poison.

Annie has regained consciousness. She slowly gets to her feet with her script. In time for her cue…

SANDRA and ANNIE. *(Together.)* I thought it was strange you got here so quickly in such terrible weather.

DENNIS. And then you found Charles' will in his ledger and tried to pin the whole thing on me.

SANDRA and ANNIE. *(Together.)* You damned crafty devil.

JONATHAN. Crafty, indeed. Perkins here is as innocent as I am. Remove those handcuffs this instant!

Robert goes to uncuff Dennis but he doesn't have the key. Robert searches his pockets for the key. Dennis remains handcuffed to the chaise longue.

Drop the gun, Inspector!

SANDRA and ANNIE. *(Together.)* Ay me!

CHRIS. Never! I came here to kill you, Charles, and I won't leave until the job's done.

JONATHAN. It's over, Inspector. I could prove your guilt in a second. I have the evidence in my study. Fetch the papers, Perkins.

DENNIS. Yes, sir.

Dennis goes to leave but he's still handcuffed to the chaise longue. He slowly leaves dragging the chaise longue behind him.

JONATHAN. Lower your weapon, Inspector. It's over.

SANDRA and ANNIE. *(Together.)* Please Inspector! You're frightening me!

CHRIS. You *ought* to be frightened!

SANDRA and ANNIE. *(Together.)* You monster! You tried to kill…

Sandra stamps on Annie's foot. Annie is hurt.

SANDRA. You monster! You tried to kill Charles and you killed Cecil! How could you!

CHRIS. I'll admit, I tried to kill Charles, but I never went anywhere near Cecil. In fact when I discovered that you and he were having an affair I was overjoyed. I had the perfect man to pin it on. Until my accomplice blundered in!

JONATHAN. It's true. And your accomplice, I regret to say, has been my friend ever since we were at school, isn't that right, Thomas Colleymoore?

ROBERT. It's true. I'm the Inspector's accomplice; I helped him move the money!

SANDRA. Brother! I'm surprised at…

Annie stamps on Sandra's foot.

ANNIE. Brother, I'm surprised at you! I don't know what you've become.

ROBERT. I'm so ashamed. I met Inspector Carter here a few months ago down at my club. We found that between us we could steal money from the police's sundry accounts easily. Carter had the access and I had the facility to move the money fast and keep it secure, or so I thought until tonight.

Robert forgets his line.

(To Trevor.) Line!

TREVOR. I don't know what page we're on mate.

ROBERT. I don't know what page we're on mate!

Robert realises this isn't the line and looks to Trevor furiously.

CHRIS. *(Whispers.) As for Cecil…*

ROBERT. As for Cecil, that was more a crime of passion, simple as that.

ANNIE. Cecil! But I loved him, he was my only…

Sandra slams Annie's face down into her folder with a thud.

SANDRA. Cecil! But I loved him, he was my only…

Dennis has now reappeared with the chaise longue carrying the papers, which he hands to Jonathan.

DENNIS. The papers, Mr. Haversham!

Jonathan takes the papers.

JONATHAN. Thank you Perkins, now fetch my cigarettes from the mantelpiece.

DENNIS. *Yes, sir!*

Dennis goes to the mantelpiece, but then realises the smoking things are offstage and he goes to get them.

JONATHAN. Now, I hold in my hand a written list of every fraudulent transaction Thomas Colleymoore and Inspector Carter made!

SANDRA. This can't be true, I won't belie…

Annie grabs the papers from Jonathan and throws them at Sandra.

ANNIE. This can't be true. I won't believe it! I can't believe it!

ROBERT. But it is true. When I found he was interfering with you Florence, my own sister, well it's more than I could bear.

JONATHAN. Your sordid affair sickened me, Florence. You broke my heart.

ANNIE. No, Charley! You mustn't, I made…

Sandra pushes Annie out of the way.

SANDRA. I made a mistake! Please, take me back! I'll be yours all over again!

JONATHAN. Take back a woman who has betrayed me? Never!

Annie and Sandra try and get closer to Jonathan, knocking him to the floor.

SANDRA and ANNIE. CHARLEY! You're all I have! Love me! Please! Don't cast me aside! I shall be an outcast in the town! My friends shan't speak to me. Never again shall I feel your embrace! Let me be your wife!

Dennis enters with the cigarettes.

DENNIS. *(Over the shouting.)* Your cigarettes, sir!

JONATHAN. *(Over the shouting.)* Thank you, Perkins! God knows I could use a smoke!

Doorbell sounds. Row subsides.

Fetch the door, Perkins.

DENNIS. Yes, sir!!

JONATHAN. That will be the police to arrest you both.

ANNIE. Charley! I cannot bear it another…

Annie grabs Sandra's ankles and drags her out through the door.

SANDRA. Charley! I cannot bear it another second! Look at me, like you used to look at me!

JONATHAN. Silence Florence! You are nothing to me now!

SANDRA. *(Managing to stand up.)* This is the worst night of my life!

Annie punches Sandra in the face; she falls out of sight behind the flats.

ANNIE. No! No! No! This is the worst night of my life!

JONATHAN. No. It is the worst night of mine.

Annie goes through the door and appears in the window, stamping furiously on Sandra's unconscious body.

But Thomas, Carter had you fooled, didn't he?

ROBERT. What do you mean?

JONATHAN. …He never intended to share the money with you! Let me summarize…

ANNIE. *(Bellows through the window.)* I LOVE YOU CHARLEY!!

JONATHAN. Inspector Carter knew I discovered you and he were both embezzling police money, so you hatched a…

Annie produces a large silver tray, which she starts battering Sandra with behind the window.

ANNIE. *I've still got the ring Charley, we can make it work!*

JONATHAN. …plan to kill me. Planting poisoned water for me to drink. Then mistakenly believing I was dead, Inspector Carter tried to pin my murder on Cecil and Florence because of their affair until your accomplice Thomas blundered in and shot my brother Cecil. Carter then tried to pin it on Perkins instead after finding my will in the ledger.

Annie has reappeared with a roll of industrial tape.

ANNIE. *TAKE ME CHARLEY! IF YOU KNOW WHAT'S GOOD FOR YOU!*

Annie begins to tape Sandra's hands together.

JONATHAN. Except what you didn't know Thomas, was that the Inspector made a nine thousand pound withdrawal from your private accounts this morning and after framing someone for my murder planned to flea, taking every penny! I think it's time to open your attaché case Inspector.

Jonathan opens the attaché case and produces several bundles of banknotes.

ROBERT. The nine thousand pounds!

JONATHAN. He allowed you to take all the risk by storing the stolen money in your private accounts. Isn't that right, Inspector?

CHRIS. Alright, it's true. I forged your signature at the bank and took out every penny. I hadn't bargained on your accountant catching on this quickly and telephoning you so soon.

Annie has subdued Sandra and made it back onstage. Robert runs at Chris, seizes his gun and points it at him.

ROBERT. You rogue! I trusted you! You made a mistake there Carter and I'm afraid it's your last!

Robert fires the gun. It doesn't fire. Robert tries the gun again, nothing. Robert tries again.

CHRIS. *BANG!*

Chris dies. Robert lowers the gun, where it explodes loudly in his face.

ROBERT. *ARGH!! My fingers!*

DENNIS. The officers are waiting in the hall, si…

Dennis knocks down the door flat with the chaise longue. Chris rolls out of the way; Robert moves back, colliding with the fireplace flat, sending that over as well. Silence. Stillness. They then quickly stand the flats back up, knocking the window flat down, leaving Annie standing in the window and revealing Sandra dazed backstage. Silence. Stillness again. Max throws snow from offstage.

The officers are waiting in the hall, sir.

JONATHAN. Excellent, escort my fiancée downstairs, Perkins. I wish to have a word with Thomas in private.

DENNIS. Yes, sir.

Dennis and Annie try to exit but can't because of the chaise longue. They end up hiding in the doorway.

JONATHAN. Thomas! You're not the man I knew from Eton, you've become greedy and jealous!

ROBERT. I'm sorry Charles, I feel as though I'm about to pass out.

JONATHAN. There's a glass of water next to the telephone.

ROBERT. Thank you, Charles! Ever the kind host!

JONATHAN. Drink it up.

ROBERT. Most kind!

Robert drinks the water.

JONATHAN. Tell me Thomas, one thing.

ROBERT. Anything, Charles. I shall tell no more lies!

JONATHAN. The glass of poisoned water the Inspector left out for me; what do you suppose I did with it?

ROBERT. Well, I don't kno… What do you mean? You don't mean you gave me the… Charley? Charley?!

He clutches his stomach and faces the audience.

No! No!! No!!

Robert dies. Max throws snow from offstage. Jonathan moves centre. Lights fade and a spot comes up on Jonathan.

JONATHAN. Oh how I wish this could have ended differently. Thomas, your lies and deceits have led you inexorably to this end. If men allow their conscience to be governed by avarice then death and destruction shall prevail. *(With finality.)* Betrayed by my brother.

A short snatch of an English new wave song like "Rio" by Duran Duran plays, then quickly cuts out.*

Cuckolded by my fiancée

House music fades in.

and almost murdered by my oldest friend. Let us hope we never again see a murder at Haversham Manor.

Fade to black.

End of Play

* See Note on Songs/Recordings at the back of this volume.

PROPERTY LIST

(Use this space to create props lists for your production)

SOUND EFFECTS

(Use this space to create sound effects lists for your production)

Note on Songs/Recordings, Images, or Other Production Design Elements

Be advised that Concord Theatricals neither holds the rights to nor grants permission to use any songs, recordings, images, or other design elements mentioned in the play. It is the sole responsibility of the producing theater/organization to obtain permission of the copyright owner(s) for any such use. Additional royalty fees may apply for the right to use copyrighted materials.

For any songs/recordings, images, or other design elements mentioned in the play, works in the public domain may be substituted. It is the producing theater/organization's sole responsibility to ensure the substituted work is indeed in the public domain. Concord Theatricals cannot advise as to whether or not a song/arrangement/recording, image, or other design element is in the public domain.

Additional Copyright Information

www.ingramcontent.com/pod-product-compliance
Lightning Source LLC
Chambersburg PA
CBHW072040070826
49504CB00042B/1197
9780822241997